I SEE

I SEE

Mystical And Other Spirited
Poetry & Poetics

Jack Shinholser

To order additional copies of this book, contact:
Xlibris Corporation
1-888-795-4274
www.Xlibris.com
Orders@Xlibris.com
38334

THE INEVITABLE

I realized the inevitable
and was a child no more;

I realized the inevitable
and was a child again.

CONTENTS

PART ONE: REBIRTH

PART TWO: GROWTH

PART THREE: LOVE

To my mother Ruby Shinholser who set me on this path.

I would also like to dedicate this book to Joel S. Goldsmith, healer and teacher, who has been my principal teacher for the past thirty years.

The truth of my existence, my relationship to other people, and the mystery of the world around me are my constant fascinations. Many times these thoughts, meditations and feelings manifest themselves poetically. These poems and poetics are my offering.

I have divided these poetic pieces into three sections: Rebirth, Growth and Love. They reflect a long period of tumultuous change and transcendence in my life. I hope you enjoy the story.

PART ONE

REBIRTH

THANK YOU, FATHER

The mysterious reality of my father's
        life was in his eyes one moment
        and in the next gone.
His eyes became like plastic doll's
        eyes, distant and vacant.
In that moment I realized more deeply
        than ever that I am
        not a body,
And this world is not a material world
        but a divine
        thought—
A thought in the creator's mind,
        which I saw
        as
A dualistic dream
        of loving and hating,
        winning and losing,
A dream of being
        lost and found,
        right and wrong.

Now I see through this mirage like I saw
      through the wisp of my father's
      life as it
      left him,
And I no longer hope for
      keener sight, but
      for vision.
And I see that miracles are not the
      transmutation of matter,
      but the transmutation of
      consciousness or mind
      from fear
      to faith
      and love.

Thank you, father, for the miracle.

MY SELF LAID LOW

Sweet exhaustion, joyous surrender,
    my self is laid low.
A powerful calming presence
    soothes my relieved mind;
In my arrogance I had relinquished
    all my inheritance,
In my defeat, the bounty of all
    creation is returned to me.

REBIRTH

Death ravages man, animal and plant,
      a merciless destroyer
      reducing tender blithesome joy
      to blackened decay and ruin,
      the lowest tone in the
      eternal symphony of life;
But this deepest resonant vibration
      is the solid foundation
      for the tiniest of all
      miracles and melodies—
      rebirth.

DECEMBER

December—stillness—a cold
  calming hush descends
  over life forces.
Down, down, seething, but down,
  quenching the passionate
  desire of fierce life,
A deep lamenting sigh as
  the cycle rescinds
  silently into darkness
To sleep, dream, sweet death,
  disintegration,
  molten regeneration,
  resurrection begins.

DAWN

A soft subtle glow builds from the horizon
      and up the open sky
As the pagent of stars fade into the dwindling
      black refrain.
Light seeps, spills and splashes down through the leaves and vines
      breaking the spell of darkness
As the night creatures cross paths with those of
      the day and
The hills lift and fold in valleys and peeks like a rumpled
      quilt from a restless night's sleep.
Incrementally, an awesome orange sun rises,
      claiming its kingdom . . . .
The day issues forth as the amniotic
      night recedes.

EGO'S HOUSE OF MIRRORS

I feel the weight of a deep frozen
    season lifting,
A reborn sun is piercing down
    to my dormant core.
There is some movement in long
    suspended thoughts,
Long accepted limitations are
    slowly melting.
I feel tiny trickles of hope
    and life within me,
Delicate visions play on the screen
    of my mind.
Change comes creeping into my
    dark inner sanctum . . . .

Change, endless change, is this
    my eternal plight?
These cycles of life and death
    have taught me nothing,
I sicken of this simplistic
    redundancy.
Leave me to my deep sweet dreaming
    of all I could be;
The raw fierce contact of becoming
    strikes terror in me.
Fear surges as I am shoved to that
    dreaded brink once more,
My claw-like thoughts cling to my
    deep inactive comfort.

Have I not stirred, performed,
      and fallen enough?
For what shallow limited intellect
      do I perform?
All that is was, and all that
      will be has been—
Only a world of posturing and
      deceit awaits me . . . .

Or could I be a prisoner of my
      own poor vision,
And is this my own ego's simple
      house of mirrors?
Often I sense a reality past
      pain and pleasure,
But my grasp is weak my vision dim,
      it slips away.

Once more I will fall into the
      sea of becoming,
Once more I will feel each degree
      of the full cycle.
Once more I will glimpse
      the truth so still,
So unchanging, so joy-filled,
      so timeless,
And perhaps this time move past this
      seemingly dead-end circle
To the sweet, victorious experience
      of surrender.

FOR ITS PURPOSES AND ITS PLEASURE

Life relentlessly pours forth
    from the microcosm,
The invisible bursting into
    glorious profusion.
Insatiably it preys upon itself
    in ecstasy,
Then as miraculously surrenders
    its spirit
    in agony
    to freedom.

MANKIND

The earth is in your hands,
     the sun is for you too;
The world is at your command,
     everything is for you.

The rivers and mountains obey you,
     the tides roll up at your feet;
Every atom of creation adores you,
     every moment of life is sweet.

Through countless lives you've ascended,
     millions of fears overcome;
Now all your doubts have been mended,
     it's true you're God's precious son.

HYPERPLANE

The day rushes along in
     tumbleweed style,
     desolate and wanting.
But in a twinkling, the muse
     flicks a spark
     into my perception.

Everything dances
     and sparkles,
Everything becomes
     light and
     arrangeable,
     transparent,
     flexible.

The twinkle eye dances
     in my mind,
The sparkle mind dances
     with my eye.
A stiff and stodgy coating
     is whisked away, and
     all creation moves,
     vibrantly alive
     and joyous.

Death and life play
     in a rollicking,
     tumbling way
Until they are combined
     into a hyperplane
     of Oneness.

THE CALLING

An elusive presence turns, twists and shadows
        through my soul—
A beguiling power beyond all concepts
        of knowledge or might,
A Power blinding the heart, mind and
        soul together,
An infinite way without mortally
        justified cause,
Irresistibly drawing the world into
        all Its forms;
A swirling kaleidoscopic veil of
        unfolding experience,
Leaving those who would to hammer
        out explanations.

It moves tauntingly, unseen, between me and
        my beloved mirror,
Prodding, jolting me as I cling fearfully
        to what I would possess.
My tortured, writhing will, snarling
        in angry defiance,
My crumbling sanity and aching limbs
        cry out for rescue,
Until, in tender awakening, I surrender
        to its mercy.

BEDROCK

Bedrock forms at the bottom of my being,
    where before there was no place
    to plant a foot.
Anger is unmasked as fear and pity for self,
    strutting, posturing, bluffing,
    diverting attention from the horror
    of my aloneness.
Childish whimpering for stroking and reassurance,
    refusing to face the unfolding truth
    of my soul's longing—
Elation when at last I find strength and grace
    enough to stand, not blinking or turning
    aside from revealed truth.

TRUTH

The mountains will crumble, but the winds
      will never wear thin;
The shores forever change, but the tides
      will never wash away;
The deserts will blaze and burn, but the light
      is unquenchable.
I too have known destruction, but love
      created me anew.

Time is a mere concept to separate
      all events,
Space, a surrealistic stage where I act
      out my dreams.
Life is a wondering path that goes
      where I take it,
But truth is a "voice" I finally
      heard inside myself.

EACH MOMENT

Out of this present moment I quarry
This stone, this rock of reality,
This moment of life.
And again, in the following moments,
One by one I quarry successive
Stones of here and now.

The past is sand and shifting memories,
The future incomplete pictures
With rosy or dark edges.
My eyes can only see what is,
And maybe past what seems to be,
But not what used to be

Or never has been.
So I act with my quarryman's will,
Here and now, until this will
Becomes a meticulous sharp-cutting
Vision of unwavering intention,
Tempered only with prayer and surrender.

DOMINION

The sun stood high above as the ferocity and insanity
     of the world raged on,
The day smiled impartial as innocence was flayed
     to its bare bones by the grotesque.
I watched mesmerized and compliant, drinking
     from this cup in frozen horror,
A thick engulfing sludge of fear, sloth, lust and
     greed had exhausted my struggling spirit.
My blunted awareness barely held the line between me
     and this nightmare.
Who or what force or influence has held my attention
     riveted to this gruesome tumult?

Then grace awakened some deeper sense of a presence
     or substance in and all around me.
A lightly dazzling barely perceptible silvery-fine
     energy enfolded me,
A shimmering exquisite white-diamonded fabric of peace,
     settled its healing touch upon me.
With gentle enlightenment I am awakened to a flow
     of transfiguring power,
An infinite super conscious, all-encompassing spiritual
     ocean of love.
My mind is lifted from the illusion of drowning in
     squalor and impending destruction,
My spirit-lighted intellect reveals my horror to be
     an empty reflection of my own mind.

I had given my dominion over my reality to
     my insatiable ego,
I was the one, the force, the influence—I had given
     my mind over to the grotesque.

AUTUMN

Time and events between seed and harvest
      bring the season to reap our dreams,
A season to gather together a gift
      of bountiful fruition,
The mystery of sun, soil, and seed transposed
      into ripened fruit,
The mystery of faith, strength, and idea
      nurtured into enterprise.
I look past these hands in humble recognition
      of their source,
And weep with thanksgiving as the rebirth
      of light, love, and joy approaches
      with the new year.

ON A BARREN PLAIN

On a barren plain somewhere in my soul,
In a dark stranded night with my body old,
With a defiant will and blood turned cold,
I keep railing at the powers against me.

In a shattered world on a shadow plain,
In a house of mirrors with a mind insane,
I curse the chaos but cling to the pain—
This is too damned absurd to be believable.

All creation is pure mind energy,
Came the thought through the wretched destruction;
I have made this ugly world that I see,
And fallen mad under its seduction.

So please, give me back my faith and childlike way,
And I promise, Creator, ne'er again to stray.

DEATH-THROES

Pounding, pounding, pounding, my feet
      pounding the earth like sledge hammers,
My driving heart slamming against
      my ribs frantically,
My ears ringing, my legs
      and body numb . . .
Today is the day I run this course
      in record time.
A terrible, sharp pain shoots through
      my leg; I've pulled a hamstring.
Falling, falling,
Crashing down, down through leaves
      sand and underbrush.
A flash of terror strikes to the core
      of my being;
The huge scaly body of a rattlesnake
      looms before me.
I feel the sting of his fangs as the
      great mouth slams against me;
He retracts himself, braces against his
      coiled body and strikes again.
My God, I can't believe it,
      I can't get away.
He pauses, his great evil head cocked
      and ready to strike again.
Gasping, I stare into his
      menacing eyes,
And struggle to control my heaving,
      exhausted body,
Hoping against hope to avoid the sting
      of another strike.

His thick triangular head, standing
      fully two feet off the ground,
Moves to and fro, eying me like
      the consummate assassin.
My quandary deepens as my brain
      grasps the situation;
My heart will pump the poison to
      itself quickly and die.
    "You evil son-of-a-bitch" I scream
      at his ugly face.
But I am held, as if in concrete,
      by his vile stare,
Terror, not venom, paralyzing
      my stricken limbs.
I am experiencing a strange connectedness
      to this devil;
I feel and hear a muffled sound
      in my ears;
A drugged sensation is taking over
      my perception.
The rattler is uncoiling in a strange,
      silent, fluid way;
He rears higher and higher and peers
      down on me.
Impossibly, he stands almost on the end
      of his tail and speaks.
    "Don't struggle, my child, the end
      for you has come;
Embrace the opening door
      to eternity."
The voice is coming from all around me,
      yet from the snake.
Without thought, I fling the sand in my
      hand into his face,
And lunge backward, flail and struggle
      in the dirt.
    "Oh, God!"

I grab at the gruesome head and fangs as
      he strikes at me again,
And seize him by the throat—he struggles
      and wraps around me.
    "I may die, you hideous bastard, but
      you're going with me."
    "Wait, sir, wait, I was wrong, you do
      not want to die,
And I beg you, sir, please do not
      kill me."
    "What do you mean?" I tighten my grip
      on his throat.
    "You only die when you wish to die, sir,
      that is what I mean,
And you have turned your death-scene
      around into mine.
Please, release me and I will reveal knowledge
      that kings would trade kingdoms for."
    "No, you lying viper, I will kill you
      before I die."
    "Please, believe me sir, you will not die; the
      illusion is broken, you are eternal."
Suddenly, I feel powerful and
      in control;
I am curious about this magical
      talking snake.
    "Okay, viper, speak and I may
      spare you."
He relaxes under my grip, and the menacing
      eyes open wide.
    "There is no world, child, there is
      no universe;
There is no God, only a
      here and now;
There is only mind, your mind,
      wake up and rule.

But, it is not the you you think
        you know,
But the you that just changed
        your destiny."
    "You mean that everything I see is just
        thoughts from my mind?"
    "Yes, but you have now interrupted your
        unconscious mind-flow,
And entered a much higher and
        more powerful reality."
    "What do you mean, there's only a here and
        now, and I rule?"
    "Your consciousness is a moving
        apparition,
And you only have validity in your
        oneness with the infinite.
You are individualized
        infinity,
And project people, places, and things
        from your deepest will.
With these apparitions, you
        vainly struggle
For the illusion of human perfection
        and happiness,
And miss the truth, that you are not
        human, but divine.
How's your grip, sir?"
I try to squeeze his throat, but my hand
        is so weak he easily slips out;
He pulls back from my stiffening body
        and gazes into my frozen eyes.
Turning, he slowly slides away across
        the dry lifeless sand.
I watch this low, low, magical creature
        and wait for oblivion.
Quietly, I lie here staring at my
        paralyzed hand
And feel a great wave
        of relief.

But, a thought comes moving over
    and through me,
Why can I feel or think
    anything?
Behind me I hear voices
    and running feet;
A hand is on me and gently turns me
    onto my back;
I am awake and alive and there's
    a deep ache in my leg.
These people are scientists from
    the university, they say,
And saw from a nearby hill what
    happened to me.
They are studying and tagging the
    rattlesnakes in this area,
And had just caught and milked the venom
    from the snake that bit me.
I was dead and this revelation has
    brought me back to life.
What has happened to me, I feel
    ancient, timeless?
These people are very kind
    to me;
They help me to get back to
    my home nearby.
My wife is frightened and takes me
    to our family doctor.
I feel within myself no resistance
    to those around me;
The words of the serpent keep flowing
    through my mind,
And I silently watch these scientists,
    my wife, the doctor,
    cars, clouds, children,
    moving before me
    like apparitions.

ROLLING-WHEEL MAN

Fast-eating, deep-sleeping, rolling-wheel man,
What kind of ludicrous deal have you made,
Your inheritance squandered while you get laid,
And beautiful gifts go unused in your hand?

Sweet-talking high-soaring rolling-wheel man,
Love hangs 'round your door, all ragged and cold,
While you mix up love potions to be sold,
Reassuring yourself that you have a plan.

Fascinated with your wheels, you are lost,
So you hide in deep sleep from the pain.
Refusing to stop, and add up the cost,
Knowing the verdict will be you're insane.

So turn the volume way up and get sauced,
And we'll watch this damned world just go
    down
        the
            drain.

THE GOD PEN

With this God pen, I focus your
        heart, mind and soul;
With this wand of syllable and phrase,
        I lace your hemispheres
        with exquisite realizations.
With this grammatical syntactical instrument,
        I slash away your ignorance and fear;
With this rod and staff of cleansing ink,
        I drag you through the blood, dreams,
        and excrement of your species
        and wash you in the squashed ruins
        of your illusions.
Until, by grace, you will see that we
        are one.

PART TWO

GROWTH

AN AUTUMN LAMENT

The pages of my existence are falling unnoticed from the
    book of life.
The flame of my youthful certainty quenched in the murky
    waters of age.
The colors of my consciousness resemble the dead fallen
    leaves beneath my feet,
And my mind squints to silence the strutting masquerade of
    celebrated fools.
Poetically, life has become for me exactly what I have
    accepted,
Exactly what "they" predicted and demonstrated for
    me.
Though humbled, I see through this sham of
    disintegration
And in courageous moments still grasp at the truth that
    taunts me,
But I struggle in vain to cast off the dead weight of my
    vanity;
Hopelessly mired in the insane belief that I can save myself
    and the world.

THE ARTIST

With the immortal brush of my soul,
I paint an infinite collage
On the canvass of my mind;
Eternal truth, translated into
People, things, and places,
Sculpting and honing the struggling,
Invisible entity
That I am.

A CALL TO LIFE

From rushing rivers to rising seas,
From thoughts to dreams,
From heaving mountains to lavish plains,
From prayers to acts,
From dormant seeds to bursting blooms,
From love to life,
From non-being to being.

Tumultuous, inexplicable circumstances to faith,
Waves to be ridden with zeal,
Heights to be scaled with verve,
A child of ever-widening opportunity,
An attitude of loving graceful nerve.

TO CREATE

To create, old and new must disappear,
Ideas and concepts are tossed aside.
Time and space discarded along with fear,
And a pure light channel will open wide.
This is no heroic effort of mine,
But a power beyond my brain's knowing.
I no longer need a map or sign,
Just surrender to where I am going.
I no longer move in duality,
I am the movement of all things together.
I no longer wonder what things should be,
But feel their essence in me forever.
I have become the hand of Creation,
A gift for all, an open invitation.

THE INFINITE VOYAGE

In the tumult of my awakening, I ebb
  and flow in a sea of thought.
Low-rolling thunderous currents lift
  and swell in my soul,
Manifesting events and people that
  course through my consciousness,
Where I clutch at and contend with
  delusions of their power over me,
Where I grapple with and struggle to
  control illusions of happiness,
Where the low, base elements in surface
  pursuits paralyze my judgment
Until contact with the true source
  of my being is forgotten
And I am near madness with fear
  and its looming horror.

Then grace, like a great globe rising
  from this spiritual ocean,
  brings healing light,
A quiet, expansive, healing calm that
  settles into peace and regeneration.

But still, another deep swell brings fear
  seeping into my vessel to threaten,
And once more this rolling, thunderous
  sea propels me forward
  on my infinite voyage.

SOMEWHERE IN HEAVEN

Today I awoke from the most
      frightening dream;
I was in a place where I was
      separate from everyone,
I seemed to be alone and separate
      from everything.
Something awful called fear ran
      through me,
And so many were haggard, and had something
      called death on their faces.
A concept called time drove everyone
      about madly,
But it wasn't really time they were chasing
      but a thing called money.
I felt the sting of cold and hunger pangs
      in me,
And I felt heavy and exhausted, and wanted
      to be held.
My spirit fell and fell, I could taste
      the tears welling up inside;
I asked for love and I got the strangest
      rejecting looks.

They were all repulsed by me and continued
        their pursuit of money.
My senses numb, my mind tortured, and
        my heart broken,
I fell into a pile of foul-smelling refuse
        and felt death approaching.
I saw glaring, angry eyes as people passed
        hurriedly by.

I awoke in agony, screaming for mercy,
        and realized
I had had one of those dreams again,
        where I think that I am something called a body.

DOWN AND BEAUTIFUL DAYS

Down
        and
                beautiful days,
Living on the wind,
        excitement and fear
                on the open road.
Time never matters,
        just the movement
                of the sun.

Shedding the scales of guilt,
        I open to all the rawness
                of raw life;
The pain, the filth,
        the shame, the danger,
I hold life to my heart
        and let it pulse
                through me.

Is this me,
        is this where I can be me, and
                peel off the sickening pretense
                        I have wrapped around me?
Night settles over the morbid past,
        and I settle for the peace
                of darkness
As I lie in my blanket
        by the side of the road
                and thank the invisible powers
                        that I have escaped
                                for one more day.

CHARMED

Music, time and mathematics wind through
    my mind and intimidate me; they,
    so perfect, I, so imperfect.
Bits and pieces of my life tumble like
    fallen leaves through my thoughts,
Time unreels so precisely I hide
    and sleep.
Pieces of dreams, bits of promises
    dappled with passion and desire,
    now withered and common,
Music and numbers mesmerize and
    I forget who I am.
Charmed like the cobra, I weave
    to and fro.
Which do I fear most, the known
    or the unknown?

FENCES

A line in the sand
An angry look
A wall of stone
A political boundary
A color of skin
A pedigree
An I.Q. score
The size of my house
A kind of car
A side of town
A bank account
A church door
A prison wall
My physical body—
Am I separate and safe or
Am I lost?

A DIFFERENT VIEW

Shafts of light slice
Through several openings
Around my room and
Converge on this one spot
Before me.
Is this some sort of
Miracle or a coincidence?
There are no coincidences
But does it have to be
A miracle?

Perhaps it is my own way
Of showing myself that
I am in control of my
Experience.
It just is.
I will be calm and
Let the creative genius
In me reveal all the
Wondrous truth I can
Comprehend and perhaps
Communicate to those
Around me.
I love my world.

THOUGHTS,

SEASCAPES AND SPIRIT

My thoughts rush before me in a great
        tide of images;
Confusing me, blinding me to the truth
        of what I am.

The rising sea rushes onto any waiting
        shore or open bay,
And the winds care not which young
        seabird they draw aloft.

But, the spirit is as true as my soul's
        unquenchable longing.
It has a perfect accounting and
        an ordered ascent;
But I only knew this was true after
        I was forced to feel it by the
        unerring unfolding of my being.

SHABBY LITTLE UNIVERSE

I sought to cross the mountains and my
    great courage, will, and brain
    bore me up and over proudly;
I sought to cross the oceans and my
    stout heart, grit, and perseverance
    bore me on sails victoriously;
I sought to cross the chasms of space,
    and the moon was handed to me
    by my great ingenuity.
But now my enthusiasm for these boyish
    adventures into the material world
    wanes, my spirit yearns for truth.
I see these are adventures to keep me
    outwardly-directed and diverted
    from my starving soul.
There are infinite balls of fire and
    clay across the universe, and I
    would never have to look at me.

But my soul hungers for the creator and
    is impatient with these endless
    diversions into more and more illusions;
The inevitable confrontation with self
    has arrived, and I must discover what
    real courage, heart, and perseverance are.
I must make the inward journey and
    slay the duplicitous dragons
    of pride and self-deception;

I must find my way through a maddening
      maze of self images created by me
      and my embraced world;
I must learn to see through these
      grandiose dreams of all my conquests
      and other ego lies;
I must stop playing God with my
      foolish little games and learn
      to see what real power is.

It is true beyond a doubt I am the
      ruler of my world but
      I am not of this world;
This world, this universe, is only a shabby
      little copy of the reality that
      I gave up to pretend that
      I could become God.

PUSH ON

Anytime I see a monolith
Just standing there,
There's something in me
That wants to push it over.

VICTORY?

Victory and defeat are mere
      punctuation marks in my
      soul's experience.
What spoils are there for me
      knowing I have vanquished
      a self-generated illusion,
And how can tears shed over
      thwarted greed move a man
      of even meager wisdom?

I seem to be an addict of tumultuous
      emotions, glutting myself on extreme
      feelings to prove I exist.
Today I vow to extricate myself
      from this ego-generated
      reality,
And open to the power, knowledge,
      and love that is beyond the
      awareness of this sentient world.

BEYOND EGO

Me . . . . you . . . . fear
      Hope
Us . . . . them . . . . fear
      Hope
Need . . . . Want
      Hope
Build . . . ownership . . . defend . . .
Dependence . . . pride . . . fall
Fear that I may lose what I have
Or not get what I want
      Anger
Rationalize . . . attack . . . war . . . murder
      Hope
Reason . . . . law
Build . . . ownership . . . defend
Dependence . . . pride . . . fall
      Disillusionment
Denial . . . anger . . . bargaining
Depression . . . acceptance . . .
      Spiritual awakening
Surrender . . . humility . . . self-responsibility
      Ego bows to spirit
Self-forgetting . . . happy . . . joyous . . . free
      LOVE
      ONENESS
      IS-NESS.

ABOVE ALL

I spread out a world
    before me,
Hung a sun up
    in the sky,
Raised up mighty men
    and nations,
Watched them live
    and die.
I unfold universe
    upon universe,
And dreams so
    heavenly,
But Oh, my precious,
    precious God,
I still hunger
    for Thee.

ONE OF MY BEST DAYS

In my life there is a rock
    on which I rest,
A rock of power, wisdom, tenderness,
    and joy.
From this foundation I see
    a boundless kingdom—
Rich plains of creation unfold
    before me,
Grand and awesome forms of beauty
    and truth unfurl.
I feel exhilarated
    and eternal.

But, there are some days I almost
    lose touch with this rock,
And crouch at its edge in fear
    of destruction;
My faith flounders and I am
    out of control.
But, another day comes and I am lifted
    on sudden wings,
Soar over my world and again rejoice
    in its grandeur.
These days are truly happy
    joyous and free.

But the best days are when I sit,
    peaceful and still,
Clear my mind of all thought, and join
    with the rock.
I see the infinite grains that comprise
    its being,
The illuminated grains that are
    released, suspended.
They are individual, but one
    with the whole.
I too am one with each grain, but still
    one with the whole.

The rock is alive, the universe
    is alive;
These illuminations are transforming
    me daily.
I am no longer in competition
    with survivors;
Sacrificial thinking ceases
    to have meaning.
I am the rock, the world,
    I am freedom.
I am wings, sky, movement,
    I am the journey.

Today is one of my
    best days.

HUMILITY

A soul came to my door thirsty,
    tired and hungry.
I took him in and served him
    as he rested.
I received far greater nourishment
    than he.

I was thirsty, tired, and hungry
    a stranger took me in.
I rested while he served me
    food and drink.
I received nourishment of much more value
    than drink, rest, and food.

Finally, I understand that God
    is omnipresent.

ALL IS ETERNAL

My eyes sweep the starry heavens,
Drinking in the infinity.
Unfathomable, but realized,
All goes on forever.

I peer into a cat's eye
And find a likeness—
Height and depth, but boundless,
All is eternal.

The sky, cat, and I, silhouetted
Against each other—
IS, is our meaning,
We are eternal.

REDEEMED BY GRACE

Out of my irresponsible thoughts comes
    the mire of my daily struggle;
Out of my arrogant mouth comes
    the design of my misery;
Out of my inconsiderate acts comes
    my humiliation.
Out of grace comes the miraculous power
    of forgiveness.

FEEDING BODY AND SOUL

My labor for today is done.
The light and I succumb
To the approaching darkness.
Softly, moods settle about me
As I rest here on my porch and
Watch gentle blues, pinks, and grays
Unfold their artistry.
My house, the trees, and fields
Become a warm secure cloak
About my body.
The chatter of my fleshly brain
Grows quiet and a window in my Mind
Opens to the Infinite One.
From within, the ecstasy of joy
And love arises.
I feel the presence that no word can name,
No thought can touch—
I am filled and refreshed.
Then slowly I descend from this
High place, and hear Carrie
Calling me for supper.

PART THREE

LOVE

PASSION, TIDES AND SAND

Desperately her waves clutch at the shore as the cold
      yellow moon drags her away.
Only hours ago she joyously pressed against these
      malleable sands in lavish joining, but
With each cycle her great soul forgets the recurring
      sorrow and joy of her imprisoning drama.
Midnight or noon I go to her as she moves in subtle or
      heaving passions toward me and this shore.
In her depths or shallows, in her width and breadth, in her
      peace or furry, I find identity, strength and joy.
In her presence I throw off the shackles of my body and
      join with her enormous, exquisite being;
My consciousness expanding past all horizons and my
      greater self is filled with certainty, love and gratitude.

IN LIGHT, IN LOVE

Light enters my eye and heart,
     I am moved,
Light shining from God's creation,
     I am joyful.
Your form, your face, your touch, your taste,
     I am immersed,
My enlivened heart and mind engulfed
     in light, in love.

BEYOND THE BIG BANG

You come walking across a
        dazzling sunlit field
        in your red flared dress,
And in my mind I am removed
        to the beginning
        of time.
I am removed to the hot
        primal center of a
        newborn universe,
And with the galaxies I speed
        from that center to the far
        reaches of creation.

Then my eyes come back to your
        beautiful strong face that
        brings me such joy,
And I realize there is no time
        or distance between
        that primal center
        and now or
        you and me.

A PLEA FOR PASSION

Oh great mystery of life hear my plea
    hear my prayer and my remorse.
Oh sweet passion, eternal flame of love,
    inspire this mortal coil of clay;
This foundering coil mired in a maze
    of self indulgence.
Forgive my errant brain that has attempted
    to cast your essence in stone;
Who has attempted to own that which can
    only be possessed when freed.
Break down the fear hardened wall to this
    bastion of resistance and regret,
Unleash your fire and cleanse my frozen heart
    of it's vainglorious icons;
Fill me with the knowledge that transcends
    logic and refines egotism into wisdom.
Redeem this arrogant fool who has ruled dark
    illusions rather than serve in the light,
Place your fiery kiss upon my languishing spirit
    and restore me to the immortality of love.

MARY

Her pictures, words, and thoughts turn in
      my mind; I struggle to understand.
Painfully, she gropes at her drawings and
      strains to ask and answer questions.
We search each other's eyes with affection,
      but pull back with caution;
Once she was almost my wife, now,
      I'm wooing her again.

She brings me fruit and cookies, we eat
      and laugh at some funny thought.
The light outside is fading; we go out
      to watch it slip away.
She pulls close, arm in arm, as we walk;
      we feel so natural and warm.
Forethought gives way to the sweetness
      of being and moving together.

It's time for me to go, she wants to be
      alone again and think.
I reach through the apprehension for her
      and our bodies respond to each other.
She flows to me, but then ebbs away in
      some doubt, some misgiving.
She's had enough, I must go; the tension
      increases steadily.
I flick my headlights at her as I drive away
      in memory of our long history together.

PEACHES

The peach tree has buds on it I noticed today,
      all fuzzy and multicolored.
Her clothing brushed my hand as she passed by me
      yesterday; I felt a little fuzzy and warm . . .
These buds sure have grown lately; they might
      pop at any time.
She put her hand full on mine the other day;
      I felt everything in me sing . . .
There's tiny fruit all over this tree; if it
      doesn't frost I'll have a bounty.
I bumped into her at lunch today and we sat
      together—was that an accident?
This little fruit is still green, but I can
      see it full and ripe in my mind.
I was all thumbs and stammers last night
      when I saw her,
She was softer and lovelier than anything
      I can describe . . .
The green is gone from this fruit; a rich ripe
      color is flushing through its skin.
As we danced last night the world stood still;
      there was only me and her . . .
Tonight, when she comes over, we're going
      to pick some peaches.

MY WORK

I feel the call, the feeling, and
      the poem begins.
I follow in a prescribed form; it
      moves faster and faster.
My poetic feet become tangled, I trip
      and stumble—
Casting away form I rush after the
      feeling and the poem.

Suddenly I ascend from my struggling
      brain to perfect mind
Instantly sailing among
      voluminous dimensions
Writing down what I can capture
      drinking in the sublime.

Then doubt pricks my ascent and
      I see my nakedness.
The poem dims, the feeling
      falters.
My detachment from concentration
      fails me,
And I begin to fall from this
      supernatural sky,
Back to earth and my primitive
      brain;
Before me on the paper, the treasure
      I have collected.
I bend over it and muse
      with joy.

A SILENT BEGINNING

I awake and all is still.
Two minutes before the alarm,
I reach out and cheat it of its frenzy.
The kitchen floor is cold, but the coffee hot,
And the gas heat is taking the chill
Off these rooms.
I hear a car speed by in the dark,
Then all is quiet again as I dress.
From my knees I speak to my creator,
And give thanks for all.
I feel a little excited as
I settle into my chair,
Anticipating my visit to
That deep silence.

I have chosen my question and
Pose it to my hungry brain.
I am comfortable in my straight chair
With my eyes closed,
And my brain goes to work expounding
All it knows on this question.
Fifteen or twenty minutes pass and
All thought is exhausted.
Finally, an infinite universe opens;
There is a deep timeless silence.

Out of this depth comes the most exquisite
Experience of love, and I receive the
Spiritual answer to my question.
I am in rapture, suspended like a baby
In an amniotic spiritual sea
Of bliss and silence.
I bask in this sublime state and let
The powerful waves of love
Move through me.

Slowly this holy current subsides and
I descend softly from the sacred
To this profane world.
A warm comforting glow goes with me
As I collect myself, close up
The house, and leave for work.
I must be there by 7:00 am.

A FACE

My life seems too much for me,
Then somehow, I've made it through the day.
I'm in the street and on the way home.
A face catches my eye.
A ray of the eternal pierces my ego's tired defense,
Love sweeps through me.
I am, I simply am.

I fixate on this precious head of a stranger—
    this window to Mind,
    eyes, thoughts,
    Creator of an infinite universe—
        created in an instant,
        lasting an eternity,
        without a moment passing.

Love enfolds me,
I am refreshed.
Home and a hot bath will be all the sweeter now.

FINGERPRINTS

I love to look out this old window
      at the pure sweet light
      on the fall leaves.
It reminds me of an old friend
      who once sat here
      with me at break time.

We worked together for years
      before he opened up
      to become my friend.
I can still see his smudged
      fingerprints there
      on the window latch,
Where he would throw his cigarette
      butts out and swear
      he was going to quit.
But he never did—it was one
      of the few pleasures
      he had left in life.

Now he's gone to a place where
      pleasure or cigarettes
      won't be a problem.
I really miss him at these odd
      moments when I look up and
      see his fingerprints there.

WE'RE VERY MUCH ALIKE

Tears strain behind my eyes,
       but I resist;
My face contorts just below
       a calm exterior.
The counselor faces Clint
       and me for our session,
       we are ready.

Weeks and cycles I've been coming
       here to heal him.
On good days he cooperates
       and strains to open.
I love this little son of mine,
       we're so alike,
       we're very much alike.

She says he won't open to
       the other children.
She says he's so into his own world,
       he won't play.
She says he doesn't realize that
       he doesn't realize.
       we're very much alike.

She asks him a question to try
       to bring him out.
I turn and squirm impatiently
       in my own thoughts.
I turn on him to rush him along,
       he's so slow.
       we're very much alike.

She wants to know about my
        impatience today;
She wants to know why I'm not
        as patient as usual.
She wants to know if, maybe
        today, I need to talk.
        I feel like him.
        we're so alike.

Without thought, pain comes tumbling
        out, comes tumbling out.
But I hold the tears, even though I want
        them to come.
I turn to see Clint has moved over
        from his chair
        to comfort me.
        we're very much alike.
        I love my little son.

ATTRACTIONS

The sweet song of a bird,
    a dash of color,
    a flutter of wing,
    a call one to another,
Heavenly bodies move in unison
    throughout the universe.
The road opens to the soul
    who yearns to wander;
A mountain rises up to the sky
    for those who would climb.

I condemn those about me for
    having my same faults;
The wounded seek out each other
    for solace and understanding;
The powerful meet to measure
    their might.

Love attracts Love, and
    fear attracts fear.
Money attracts money, and
    light attracts life.
Time attracts those who would be
    immortal in this coil of clay.

You inspire Love, life, and joy in me—
    I am attracted.

LOVER'S PLEA

The diffuse, smoky, shades of twilight
    settle outside my window
    and around my heart.
The sounds and smells of these rooms
    bring back your memory
    in this blue, blue moment,
The white heat of my anger, pale
    and weak now, juxtaposed to
    this aching emptiness.
Oh, love, please sense and feel my
    sorrow, and for our oneness,
    and in our oneness,
    come back to me.

COMMITMENT

The guests mill about in anticipation
       of the ceremony;
I ignore any doubts my heart may
       be feeling.
I've watched her prepare herself for days
       with calm certainty.
I know her well but she is still
       a mystery to me.

The man asks for the ring to be put
       on her finger.
I look in her eyes and see
       a quiet resolve.
For years we have forged
       this commitment,
And now I see it in her eyes
       and feel it in my heart.

The love that passes all understanding
       is fulfilling itself in us today.
       "I do."

I USED TO THINK LOVE

I used to think love was my mother telling
    me that I was more important to her
    than anything else in the world,
    but she let my father abuse me,
    day in, and day out.
I used to think love was a woman telling
    me that she could not live without
    me, but then I found out that I
    was a blank face she was using
    to fill a hole in her soul.
I used to think love was my best friend
    telling me that he would be there
    for me, no matter what, and then
    I found out he was trying to
    take my wife.
I used to think love was my child coming
    to me for advice and help, until she
    put me in this nursing home, and
    never comes to see me.

Now, I know that love is keeping the
    first commandment:
"Thou shalt have no other gods before Me."

SECRETS

One secret afternoon she came with
      her power and her mysteries.
She is three years older and far,
      far wiser than me.
She spoke to me softly, but I felt
      very unsure about her;
For days she's been coming here telling
      me stories and secrets.
One day out behind the shed, she told
      me where babies come from.
She wants me to go with her, she has
      a special secret to tell me.
But what will she want me to do?
      what will she do to me?
She took my hand, led me to the
      closet in the back room,
And buried us in the dirty clothes
      on the floor there.
She told me more secrets about what
      grown-ups do in the bed at night,
And put her hand on my private parts.
      I lost my breath.
Why won't she leave me alone? Why is
      she doing this to me?

LOST INNER CHILD

Dark sullen injured gaze,
Anger and fear-stained face,
Provoked exposed trembling
In the shunned light, naked.
Encouragement falling with a dull
Thud on paralyzed emotions,
Sheer terror like razors threatens
All moves toward freedom.
Still the child steadfastly
Holds against certain disaster,
Reaching for
      my hand
      my faith
      my trust
      and my love.

REACH THROUGH

THE DARKNESS

In a thoughtless moment, I was abrupt
        with my sweetheart;
I hadn't noticed the tight, strained
        smile on her face.
In a flicker, a dark cloud passed
        over her features,
And I recognized that dreaded
        intruder, depression.
With a foolish remark, I tried to
        deny its presence,
And she scathed me with quick, sharp
        angry words.
I felt shame as she turned stone-like
        and walked away.

Later, she sat gazing out her
    open window.
I asked her if there was any way
    I could help?
The dual faces of an angry woman
    and a frightened child
Turned on me and plumbed the depths
    of my sincerity.
I shrank inside from the power
    of her awesome challenge;
My love seemed so frail in the face
    of this dark presence.
But, steadfastly I held to the
    truth of my love,
And with my heart, reached through
    the darkness for her.

LOOKING IN

Through a fence of crippled emotions,
    I gaze at a garden of love,
People touching, laughing, crying,
    holding each other.
I am denied what I can see and almost
    reach out and touch;
I try to accept a simple offering of love,
    but fear seizes me.

My mind and heart careen in anguish
    and desire,
I am flooded with silent screams
    of anger and shame,
Paranoia perverts this simple offering
    into the grotesque,
Kindness, hope, and acceptance are
    twisted into evil.

I back away constricted, yet steeled in
    the safety of my condemnation;
The fear ensnared in my flesh has again
    stifled the screams
    of my soul
    for love.

OUTRAGEOUS

Open up! Open up your mind and legs
      to my creative seed.
Expose your tender underbelly to the
      cleansing fire of simple truth.
Wager the fear and anger matted on your soul
      and eating at your nerve endings.
Dive to the pooled center of your outrageous
      righteousness and bargain for
      your ears and voice.
Then, come lie down with me and we'll
      pull the warmth of the universe
      up under our chins
      and dream.

AUTHOR

Jack Shinholser was born in the small farm community of Blakely, Georgia. He spent most of his early years in and around Tampa, Florida and attended Florida State University on a football scholarship. In his senior year he was named second team All-American by the Newspaper Enterprises Association, All American-honorable mention-Associated Press, All American-honorable mention-United Press International and received many other honors.

Mr. Shinholser retired from the Tennessee School for the Blind, located in Nashville, TN, in 2002, and he and his wife Verma moved to Orlando, FL where he is pursuing his writing of short stories, novels and poetry. Mr. Shinholser has two sons, Richard, who is career military in the United States Air Force and Clinton, who lives and works in Lebanon, TN.

If you have enjoyed these pages, please help this striving poet by sharing my book's website with family and friends.

Printed in the United States
91524LV00004B/33/A